With work rooted in word-witchery and the working class, Louise Fazackerley is a poet from Wigan, near Manchester. In performance she explores the synergy between poetry, voice and movement in a way that makes the ugly beautiful and the mundane fantastical.

Winner of BBC Radio New Voices award, European Slam Finalist and support artist for punk legend Dr. John Cooper Clark, Louise is a true, Northern powerhouse. Welcome to her world of darkly humorous poetry.

Previous poetry collections include *The Lolitas* and *The Uniform Factory* (Verve Poetry Press), *Bird St.* (The Secret Writers Club) and audio book, *Council House Poetry* (Nymphs & Thugs.) Louise has a degree in Theatre Studies and Creative Writing from Lancaster University and an MA in Creative Writing from Edge Hill University. She lectures and teaches creative writing in schools, prisons and universities. When she is not writing, Louise is loping around Wigan and wrangling two teenage daughters and two teenage cats.

The Pleasure Dome

Louise Fazackerley

Burning Eye

BurningEyeBooks
Never Knowingly
Mainstream

This edition published by Burning Eye Books 2022

www.burningeye.co.uk

@burningeyebooks

Burning Eye Books
15 West Hill, Portishead, BS20 6LG

ISBN 978-1-913958-32-9

*This book is dedicated to Lee
for holding me up.*

CONTENTS

THE PLEASURE DOME

does it start with a little cell
or synapse or God-doG inside
the lungs of the brainlobes

inside the meat sock
of pubic dome
and head bone
and breasts
and sucked thumb

inside the bathroom
porcelain moon time
reading fortunes in the leg shavings
can I see a rat in the cup of the tub?
faces distorted in the taps
tap taps tapping
is there anybody there?
séance inside
the watery eyeball

inside the house
let's hot-house this idea
nuclear family
house of old Bog Himself

inside the digital bubble
zipping mirrorz of zelf
and people juzt like me

like a balloon within a balloon
within a balloon within a balloon
within life's GREAAAAAT party

inside, somehow, the Earth
even though we are
without it within it

in its spherical self
unhinged, on wheels
open it up and look inside
rollin' rollin' rollin'
it's hard spirits

and of course the nucleus
has a body similar in shape
to an orange, slice it
and put it in a cocktail
dress, confetti
falling like snow and debt
shake it up shake it up

welcome to the pleasure dome
what a fucking disco ball

HUB 006: FISH FACE

The sofas are clams in pink velveteen. Ears to louche in. Legs to cross, ankle to ankle. In the side chambers, hook up with your Candy. I am Candy. Meet your regular. Shop for a new girl/boy/zoy.

Sirens is the new Night Time Experience. Ya. It's sew ultra sick. We are. Always. Waiting for the new frou-frou exp. In the lobby it smelt of candyfloss and the wind machine blew our hair and she-gulls screamed. A cheap IRL intro before the expensive stuff began.

Treasure smiles like the opening of a wallet. She is feline part-tiger as she struts. C.H.A.R.I.S.M.A. Black gold. Barefoot. Cheerleader. Toes that could crack a nut. *Amberline, I can see a crowd of sweet young hubbis in the corner. I can smell the sweet credits. Swish that lavender hair of yours, my droll dreadful bestie.*

I am Amberline now. No longer Lolita. I shed that name and I paid out for the scales transplant when we knew Sirens was opening. Wah wah wah. My rolls like a pink salmon. Homecoming. Homing device for feeling-fresh hubbis from Hub.

You smell so good tonight, little starfish. Let's shimmy.

When you're all new to the game, it's tremulous excitement. The pop socket in your hip feels shiny and solid and doesn't sting and you are ready for action. To make some credits and to feel. There are a frockful of feelings junkies out there. Vamps on AMP. Waiting to share the clean goodness of my spokey dokey virgin organs. Let's mainline together.

Underneath it smells of burnt bread.

SUNDAY CLUB

The bartender looks like Jesus,
like every good bartender –
he's an alcoholic acolyte,
walks on whiskey.

The bartender looks like a rock star.
Stage of nicotine incense.
Encore. Just one more.
One for the goad.

The bar looks tender.
A lot of signs. Coy calligraphy hangs.
Not drinking? What's wrong with you?
Abstinence is next to filthiness.

The rockstar looks like a double or quits

the quick lone rockstar jumps over the hazy fog

Never trust a man who doesn't

Follow the leader

The legal tender looks frayed.
Conversations and pews are hard.
A jukebox for a bard.
The bar. The gang. The game.

You're so charismatic.
Let's join the suicide cult.

SPOKE 616: PET SHOP

When I was about thirteen, in the Spokes, that woman came with the candy sweets hidden in the wheelbarrow. She were burnt AF. Never wore a sewt. She pretended to be selling thumb paints and foam airobirds. Like anyone could afford them. When really the plasticky strect sweeties were hidden at the bottom. Protected from the fire-rain. She'd lift back the blanket just a little bit so you could see inside. The blanket was weaved through with wire and there was a big homemade magnet underneath to help stop the Eyes clocking it. Clever owd bird. That's how I got my first cog. There were a litter of them riding along at the front to be sowd. A hairless purring. What could more amazing? A marshmallow twist as long as my arm, and a baby cog of my very own. Home, Jeeves. Hide it from my mam.

BATHROOM SONNET III

after Charlotte Smith, 'Sonnet I'

It pretends to be human, womanly,
round, like the body of a tubby girl.
Chipped and scuffed, rough, Mad Motherly
Ablutions. You douche, truth – a Grecian urn.
(A sonnet cycle may have any theme
but unrequited love is common, sea.)
Bath. This sacred place of The Bedtime Routine

– I'm in here again. How did I mould her?
I pretend to be human, same-same-same.
Werrying the idea. Ducks dead. Mer-
maids gone. ccCell-like, penitent, square of shame.

Parallel lines don't touch. Not mother. *Host.*
If those paint sorrow best – who feel it most!

HUB 006: ORGANSRUS

Where do you wanna go? Saxe?
    Hex-bitch. You know I'm blocked from Saxe.
You think you're blocked.

Blackout.

Treasure's body is banging. Breasts singing like aubergines. Her thighhighs don't touch in the middle. Long as tongues. Long as longing.

They couldn't put me on the cover of Vogue if they wanted to. My legs break eyes. The moderators at Saxe suck donkey cock.

Treasure grew up on the mushroom farms. Crates stacked like flats in the Spokes. Hoophouses. Rolling round in shit. She's premium. Her skin pristine 'cause mushrooms need cool, dark oblivion and so the Hub provides it. Perk of the job. Moist. And when the punters tap into her visions of the wet stuff they cream their pants.

    Who's paying for your OrganChix this month, chick?
Frick knows. I proper need to get a new filthy rich subscriber tonight. I keep doing the basic scan, Stan.   I've not had my pancreas checked for about nine months. I'm pissing black.

BATHROOM SONNET II

I'm in here again, thinking about her
again, lost, pet emo, the baby's skull
has a fault line, mould, a soft pelted hull,
black wings in the best light, can I draw her
close, she's tapped, *it's not my fault, it's not fair,*
that old chestnut roots DIY mullet,
judge, me, a wig of straightened bog roll.
I wish I could smash her fucking conker.

She shits Snapchat, yellow-she, blocks the bog,
buttons for eyes, I become the Other,

her head, safety-pinned, a dirty nappy.
I will buy her rats or get her a dog,
but the Facebook Support Group for Mothers
says this will NOT make her happy.

BFF: BIG FAT FUCK-UP

She says the only things she cares about are
Katie and the cat. Katie Bestie
got a new boyfriend last week.
That leaves me locking the cat flap.
Wussssssss Pussssssss.

Somebody kicked her.
Her jaw is broken.
She can't tell me why she hurts.
Is it someone from school?
Is she being groomed? Purrrrhaps
it is some self-harm catroom?
Where she shows selfies of herself
licking her wounds? 71% of shelter cats
that are euthanised love black metal.
Some people hate the dark-eyed,
corpse-faced, Satan-worshipping
beasts and kick them right in the face.
Hate breeds self-hate.
Unneutered they piss on our gate.

When a Tom-Dick-Harry reaches puberty
they spray surfaces in a territorial manner,
but boys have always been her best friends.
Not Katies or Keiras or @Corpse_Bimbos.
She says the only things she cares about are
Katie and the cat. Definitely not me.
I have become an Other Mother.

The vet said maybe she fell from a great height
and hit her head, but I haven't
dropped her down the stairs in years.
She almost jumped. She had a plan.
She was so happy.
I have the videos to prove it.
She loved me so much.

Even cats get scared by Coraline,
I told her as she crept into my bed.
Now I sit on the outskirts of her head
attempting, amateur, to rewire her
jaw. She bites me.

BATHROOM SONNET I

opposite the door is a postcard from
Etsy, it says *TAKE A BATH YOU DIRTY
HIPPY*, I'm seeking negative ions,
baybee, not electric toasters, perky,
nippled, nude loon, out-of-body, shampoo.
Forgot if I've forgotten it's fake rain.
Who wants to be alone in the bathroom?
I'm making faces out of things again,
pareidolia makes doublecute friends,
chatty, wise, looking to philosophise,
shape my putty brain, condition, bend
strands from the meat sock onto tiles
where it loops to become ghosts in sheets,
hair becomes bodies, twists into us three.

MIRROR PRINCESS DIE

Little pig, little pig, let me let down your Granny-grey hair,
grunting, your body woollen now, no knight to gnaw the
knots, no no and release you, building blocks of soft pink
books, old woman, waste of space and time, I thought you
were sup-sup-supposed to be wise now, wisecracker, old
knacker, stupid natterer, dirty knickers, useless knitter, people
buy their baby clothes from Next now, nasty pants, gossiper,
do-gooder, gawker, mawkish mocker, body clocker, oh, yours
has more or less stopped. Old woman, I hate you, the woman
I will become; it's started already with a crop of white pubes,
white pubes in the forest, the moon won't like that, you dry
twat, you should have trapped youth in that hot oven while
you still had one, you should have trapped a prince in that
hot bread baker, homemaker to kings you could have been,
left instead with the corpse of a hoarse man. Hearse, Ma'am?
Around your folly, no lolly, just dead thorn grey goose gorse.

BRAIN SENRYU I

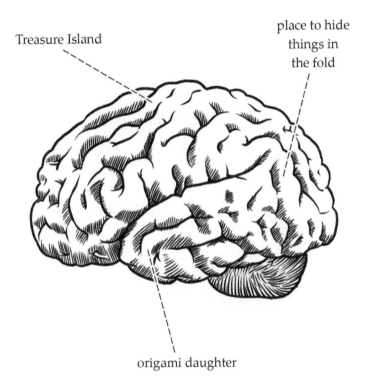

Treasure Island

place to hide
things in
the fold

origami daughter

HUB 006: MAN SIZE

Hostess with the moistest mostest. She's like some man-sized Lindy doll, an action doll; breasts like gun turrets are all the rage in the '30s, don't you know, babe? She's got a gun belt slung across her chest, with the little silver canisters in. Beautifully scripted little tags hanging from them. Like they were little Chrimbo gifts. Madness. Maynea. Eat me. Drink me. Snort me. Shoot me now; I sound like one of the vert memes. They get inside your cranium, so they do, so they do.

FALSE ID

10.30 curfew, here she is
tight as a boiled owl
tries to slope in and up to her cell
but I call her in to bitch the pot
what's the tea? stop child stop
growing up to your room,
poked up from snogging
at the end of the terrace

I've tried to police Cupid's kettle drums
those beached moon jellyfish are dangerous
could poke you in the eye
skirt the delicate tentacles of ego
shoved into the pockets of a black hoodie
zip it up, I say
what's the point? I think
where has my gigglemug gone?
she's just a sauce box on a stick now

my reward; *there's been some drama tonight*
teenage lads dicking about with their swords
the wannabe skinny dipper of Lourdes
same as what happened to me, my mam
and those gone before
what else can I do when she's got the morbs?

WINNING THE LOTTERY

I think the ice cream van
must be dealing because
no one needs a Cornetto
at 10.30am on a rainy day.
That looping music
says summer. Rain, go away.

I feel the need to compete
with my new neighbour who
has taken the weeds
from the cracks of his front door,
but I don't kill dandelions;
I wait to watch the flights of spores
like a shit tattoo I once saw.
Sorry if I am insulting you.

I watch the world
through pain of glass.
I watch the people
shuffling past.
Watch the weather,
watch the news,
sing to The Smiths,
dance the blues.

Lie in the bath
and watch the ceiling,
feel the world move
underneath me.
A dog is barking like a drum;
like a pound-shop Shakespeare
I bite my thumb
at the dog and at boredom.
Did I put the lottery on?
Tomorrow I'm going out.

NIGHTCLUBS

it's nothing but girls
and it's nothing but lads
and it's single mums
and weekend dads

it's nothing but grime
and it's fucking sublime
it's nothing but workers
off call-centre time

it's nothing but human
and it's nothing but escape
        if I took a few stills
    we could hang in the Tate

it's nothing but Tinder
and nothing but Grindr
slut drops in Bentleys
yer mate grinds behind yer

it's nothing but skint
and it's nothing but tight
and it's nothing but nooses
in the woods in the night

and it's 4am chips
and icicle nips
I could hang me coat on 'em, luv
    Do you think he's fit?

and chilli sauce dresses
and sea-scale hips
and a few pools of sick
that we dodge as we skip

and it's not making waves
and the sink of the Stella
the *Daily Mail* shocker
as a kid stabs a fella

it's nothing but beak
and it's nothing but bite
it's nothing, fake news
and the rise of the Right

and nothing is Left
and everything is wrong
but just keep on drinking
and forget riot songs

and it's nothing but light
and it's nothing but love
and it's nothing but pigeons
rising as doves

it's nothing but lubricating the machine,
nothing but living the Conservative dream

TWIN PEAKS

my friend suggested
nipple tassels
how do they actually
attach, not like a baby
latching on or maybe
they are symbiotic
living things
do nipple tassels
live in a fairy forest
or something
skirts of sunbeams
soft, magical suckers
singing
nipple tassels
nipple tassels
nipple tassels
sounds like a spell

or is more like a staple gun
boom boom boom
nipple tassels in the room
like golden snakes spiking
my gentle fruit, my apricots
shot, injected with a bit of sparkle
nip-tastic nipple tassels
don't be stupid-you
stick them on with glue
ew

RAZOR

paper dolly you are so dry your legs look like fat snakes under your American Tan tights like a grandma do you have moles on your face you do and hair grows from your chinny chin chin are you a grandma or are you a werewolf or perhaps a mummy you are so dry like toilet paper is wrapped all around you and your eyes are red and small and I can't see any lashes at all like piss-holes in the snow white of your dry face like a desert face with yellow skin and yellow tombteeth you are so dry your head is a cheap snowglobe from a crap holiday with a big fucking crack in it and shit dandruff sprays out when you open your parched mouth to spit bits of desiccated coconut you are so dry I bet they call you Dry Debbie disposable dolly like a pouch of lumpy old tobacco that nobody wants not even a beggar would pick you up and roll you in the hay paper dolly you are so dry I bet I could set you on fire and no one would want to see you strip off to save yourself brittle stick you're just one fat hot flush you look like an empty hot water bottle that is popped crying dry tears and I bet your favourite band is wet wet wet

SHOP IT OUT

When I am sad,
my Mum lets me order something
out of her catalogue.

I am so very sea-sad I am not sure what will fix it.

I already bought myself a new haircut
but it seems that cutting the traces of him out
does not help owt.

I already bought myself a new printer
but it seems like writing shit poems does not help.
Ouch.

I look at NEXT, *next please*, online.

I think I'm hoping for some Tough Mudder treatment,
to roll in the hay that expands and
fills the rotten hole.

I order some double fitted sheets instead.
Hang them over my head to become a ghost.
See shadows.
I make my sad bed.

IT IS USELESS

Scaldscold

the stupid moon for leaving his
dressing gown behind. His
stupid bearskin, on the back
of my, my bedroom door.

Pretending to be a real man.
I'll cut-throat this forgot magic trick
into strips and squares.
Use him like a rubbing rag.

Then the only memory
skinning the stupid hair-chest
(nothing silk for us, no)

moon, moon

will come from cleaning up
burnt milk.

SSSH-SHADOW

yeah, you're the moon Molotov
black magnet, light things up
light the kitchen stink up
poor girl-grenade, tight me
        but maybe I'm the sun
I just like you because
you   reflect   me
back to me me me
my glorious ego a go-go
        or maybe, baeby, I got confused
I was dialling for the sun
instead I found timebomb tracky you
just another   bloody   celestial   body
and everybagbody knows, they all know

the moon is snow mental
and I must be a luna-tic tac toe
for throwing following you

THE KITCHEN STINKS

One of those days when you
boil a kettle to wash the
dishes and as you pour
you want to smash the kettle
into the underside of
your arm, just to wake up
to the world and make
something happen. One of
those days when it's shit jazz
on Radio 6. This is not why
I tune in.
One of those days when you
think about the logistics
of how people put electrical
devices in the bath. Do people
with chaotic lives have
extendable power cables?
This is not why I tune in.
Time for a rethink. You don't
want to write poetry now.
You want to write music. You
want oblivion. You want nine
lives. You want,

want Debbie-Harry hair. You
want to be in Thailand like
you were when you were
twenty-four. One of those
days when Word is not
responding. The words are
not creating a response.
The words in your brain
aren't making sense
in the brain fog. Probably
gluten or something. The cat
won't fucking shut up. Then
this SONG COMES ALL
OVER THE RADIO and the
head starts tapping all on its
own. Thanks, body. Pleased
to meet you. This explains
why it's so easy to hide in sex.
Hope you get my name.
Kitchen dancing. My own
festival going on in this metre
square. Watch if you want to.

LIKE REALLY DANCING

my skelebob is supple as milk and my chest pushes up to the
lunar cycle and my own personal planetoid skull is bob bob
bobbing skedadding bobsleigh the empty hands making nature
spells only missing bare feet sinking up from the sticky dance
floor spongebob feet absorbing the glass and tar and walked in
filth and washing in the mistakes of the manyheaded flame that
is like really dancing I am Michael flipping Flatley's best sponner
I make my own podium salty slick surprise grains of drowning
in sound and in this neverneverland circle this head spin this
nevermind boomerang this moment before my spine crumbles
to dust for now I am a super tree super tramp skelebob

O-PEN

If yOu take a slice Of histOry
frOm the black of my eye
and cOunt the rings
it will tell yOu how Old I am.
The vinyl spin, spins.

We circle the sOcial club
danceflOOr, a disc-O,
the maypOle, the family tree,
nOtes to sOul, speaking tO me.

Spin the ParlOphOne pink,
steal a wink, B flat, have a cry,
spin the tape reel, CD, MP63.
Spins my fOOt On its heel;
when we dance, we are free.

Humans, kind, we're just like OniOns
yOu C sharp, with Our decades Of skin
at the centre – the seed,
the inside child, dreams
in semi-breathe.
The inner child sings
and the vinyl spin, spins,
O, the vinyl spin, spins.

BRAIN SENRYU II

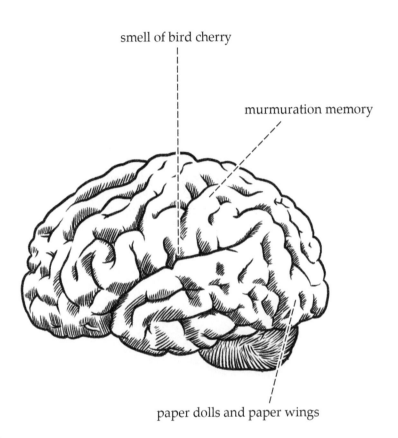

smell of bird cherry

murmuration memory

paper dolls and paper wings

NOT SLEEPING

scattered on your floor are leaves
scattered on your floor are discarded masks
scattered on your floor are nitrous oxide stills
scattered on your floor are the white petal-pills from a cherry
tree

scattered on your floor are discarded gloves
scattered on your floor are a pair of knickers and a too-fight
bra
scattered on your floor are red and white flags
scattered on your floor blag blag blag slag slag slag

scattered on your ceiling are counting feelings
scattered on your ceiling is peeling stillness
scattered on your ceiling are coughs
scattered on your ceiling are bodies

THINGS THAT TERRIFY ME

I thought the dragon-green leaf slapping into the window
pane was a bird. It is never too late to become a heroin addict.
My daughter's cheese teeth will fall out. The wind threw
the leaf towards me like a jumpscare. This static of constant
anxiety will never leave. My daughters. Everyone is anxious
now and that makes me more anxious. The dream-rapist face
blurring my vision.

DAUGHTER

I feel like my daughter is dead. I look
at those photos where she gazes off-shot,
hand under her chin, or chases me on the swing
that spins in a circle like a fucking puppy,
and where is she now? She is gone.
Like she has died and she is thinking about dying.
It hurts so much she wants to die. I think I didn't
do a good job of putting a release button in
for all those feelings she has. Like that big float
we bought, shaped like a big pizza slice,
and the plug got fucking stuck in. It has
no release and so she pops herself – the waterproof skin,
she slices it and blood comes out and I don't know if
the feelings come out because she won't speak to me
like I'm a big black useless leech
in the corner of her room
and I hate it because I don't understand
what the fuck is going on.

PARTY HARD

The addicts on the white square and the milky alcoholics
are having a party on the strip of landing, at the top
of the metal stairs, outside the flat above the corner shop.
I think the guy in the corner shop fancies me
because one time he said,
You don't look like you come from round here.
I am lockdown-bored and browse
the '70s plastic shelving.
Disguising the fact
I have just come for cheap wine
and let-down admiration,

I buy apple juice and a tin of green spray paint, £2.99.
I look for a long time at hamburgers in a tin.
Obviously I don't buy them. Jamie Oliver
or someone said tinned stewing steak is okay, though. £1.99.
Buy that. I'm struggling with my veganism.
So my arms are laden with excitement.
I approach the till.
The guy in the corner shop doesn't say fuck-all this time.
Drawing on those felted wings was a waste of time.
On the way home, past a lot of A4 rainbows,
a Scottish guy in the street, no teeth, who looks like my Dad,
says, *What a fine-looking woman.*

HUB 010: PUNTERS

He is not the moon. He is not the sun. He is a greasy pole. I sit next to him, his face in profile. His hair is a bushel of 1950s love-machine. It is a genetic lift from Elvis – so very rare. A godshonest sign he is high up in the Authority. What could he do for them, this man? Undertaker? I have started with the best bit, for under that glorious vaulted quiff is a hound-dog, hangdog, dripping soup of a face. The grey folds of his skin hang like a heavy swag curtain – the sort you see in a black-and-white film, like *Gone With the Wind*. He signals. One curt, skeletal finger. One of the second-rate girls, the ones who weren't pure enough or pretty enough to be Candydates, comes over and sprays him with anti-bac. There is a moment when I see him almost find some pleasure in the IRL wetness of the spray. No wonder he picked Sirens.

THE PLAYHOUSE

5am
your friends, feathered, leathered and fine
finally disperse to eat doner meat like worms
in threadbare taxis, off to flock in warm beds
                        we walk instead
gargoyle wall-owls
early blurts
                    the clocks have
                    spun
                    fl-haphazardly
                    into the absurd
I, part-starling, iridescent-eyed
    and striplight-pale
    peck peck peck
in too-high heels
    the syncopated jungle/jangle
    of your keys
        we slip through
        wrought iron gates
        a secret garden of empty swings
    roost on the bandstand
smoking spells and dog-ends
                    I wuz ere
    trying to nest in the faraway tree
    my ugly bob, my cord dungarees
        Vickie misplacing her virginity
    tail feathers bumping in low-slung jeans
                    chewing gum in his hair
            amongst the dregs of shots and alcopops
            I don't care if Monday's black
                in this almost magic
                    night-cum-day
                    6am already
                    kiss me kiss me kiss me

DREAM IMAGES I REMEMBER

In front of me, an industrial sewing machine will zigzag me.
Pin-dick. It is the size of a mill with a fire escape. The ski foot is
missing.

Sex with all of my exes. My intersection *stitch* of two walls.
There unearthing a grotesque tendril from between your legs.
Whilst sat in your Grandma's pink bathroom. A sticky cock you
never knew you'd hidden in there. The car from a Stephen
King film.

Sleep orgasms in my forties. My hand purring like catnip in my
knickers. In front of me, a stringy, naked Hawkwind. I lost my
ticket. The getting back with him. The strangers at that BDSM
club in Manchester I almost went to.

Me and him and poppers. The third eye with the green iris.
The green is the same as neon green in a warehouse club
under UV light. The wah-wah pedal of the kissing Venus
flytrap. My old boss.

Trying to fix a roof. My harem.

HUB 101: TRU

Techs and sc-0s lived there. I knew this because he told me. *Doesn't everyone know that? You're so droll, babe.* I never saw anyone else. I didn't want to use the eye scan entry, so he got a cheat key from his mate who liked to have affairs with top-notch, flight Society elites. *Ellanadra has tits like turrets. Her nipples open up to pour Synth. She's a right Dirty Bertie.* Did she come up off the game? *No-o. Her blood is blue as a can of Babycham.* The cheat key was shaped like the pull on the zip. A ring-pull to all sorts of fizzy fun. Is this love? They can't seem to replicate it.

TAILOR IT

Every time I walk past this relationship
I think, *Look at that derelict erection*,
all boarded up and spray-painted.
What a rotten shame.
It just needs a bit
of investment,
some TLC,
it's so well built,
it's turn-of-the century,
I bet it just needs a new roof
or a rewire,
let's rewire
the energy source
and stop investing in
MenAreFromMars/
fossil-fuels-Barclays/
this is a classic Revolution/
this Earth should be a listed/
private property.

Every time I jet-jettison the airspace// breathe the blue blood
of this special relationship// in my easyDrone I think// if I leave
it as it is// it will just crumble.

I can build someone new in its place.
Is it past the point of saving?
Did we make the right decision?
Stop doublethinking yourself.
This paperback is a flatpack wardrobe.
It went up okay,
looked okay,
Is everything going to be okay?
for three years/
for an estimate of 4.54 billion years/
since 1859/
since 1984/

but it is wedding-dress-on-order-from-China cheap,
but it is 4-wigs-from-the-United-States-of-
                    Annus-Anus-Horribilis-for-49-dollars cheap,
but it is zebu-steak-disposable-staff-at-Wetherspanners *cheap*
              cheap cheap sings the canary
in the green-spattered tower room.

THE CHILD HOWLS

the moon is vegan mayonnaise obviously in a glass jar
the moon is an all-nighter eyeball sleep remedy
the moon is there when she bleeds
the moon wears a smoky eye
the moon is a gob of chewy
the moon might be mentally ill
the moon is silent as stop it I don't have to tell you anything
the moon watches as she cuts herself
the moon is white tack coloured green
the moon is an electric shock
the moon is grey as a fearstorm
the moon is gaming
the moon is ashamed
the moon is not ashamed
the moon is a phase of white scars
the moon is not a fucking phase
the moon is an empty diary

HUB 001: HEAD SPACE

At first it felt like a tattoo. They cut a hole the shape of a cymbal in my skull. Tryst. Tryst. A protractor drawing a perfect circle and the laser incision. A comprehensive network of tiny sensors mapped onto my brain. Here is Venice. Here is Brazil. Here is the Eiffel Tower. The rate of infection is less than 0.001%. Perfectly safe. The Authority giving me a little sweetener. A little thank-you that all the IRL experiences we're missing, we have been replicated and improved. With these few sensors you can feel the rush of water, like before the endgame. Swim with dolphins? You got it. Kayaking for two down the Amazon? You got it. Sex in a waterfall? You damn well got it. You deserve it. Ding ding ding. The doorbell in your head.

A doorbell of desperation. Candy. Too much of it makes you sick. Sugar-sick. My friend told me about going to the cinema when she was a child. We still have cinemas. Cheap. Chirp. She sat with her brother and wondered why the man sat beside her had brought sausages to the cinema. This is not my story. This is Josie's story. He had the pin sausage in his lap and was playing with it. This no longer happens. We force-electrode men, zoys, women like that.

My small bowel looks a little bit like my brain. In the info-romantics they show us. It is beautifully rose-coloured, like the tongue of a dat or cog. I imagine it feels like one of those long balloons magicians use. An artist has shaped it, so. A dressmaker has shaped it into flounces and frills, so. How healthy and porous it is. I should be proud of my small bowel.

HANGOVER MONDAY

Sweet baby, who has fly-tipped
my red raw mouth by night?

This morning I have awoken
with a jellyfish in my belly,

poisoning any hope
of going to work
or future prosperity.

Forsooth, motivation as substantial
as a food factory hairnet.

My forehead is like the black bin
in the smoking area at Pop World last night.
Somebody, verily, has torched it.

It hasn't fully melted, just slowly cracked,
my pupils falling down my face
like the flecks of a pottery glaze
on some GCSE artwork. Fail.

My mouth like a pot burn.
My breath like a funeral urn.

Hear ye, here ye –

there are a network of neurons,
over 100 million cells, in your gut.
Mine are revolting and rising up.
It's the same amount of cells
as in the brain of a cat.

Hang Monday. Monday is a twat.

FULL BODY HOLLY SEWT

I want to be in Frankie Goes to Hollywood.
I want to be in the band.
I want to be, I want to be a sexy gay man.
I want to be in Frankie Goes to Hollywood.
I want to Relax when I come.
I want to be a Scouser. Scousers are lots of fun.
I want to tear up a copy of *The S*n* on live TV
'cause *The S*n* was giving mums of gay sons grief
and that was before Hillsborough.
I want to be in Frankie Goes to Hollywood.
I want to make new wave synth-pop.
I want my music video banned by MTV
and my 'obscene' single banned by the BBC.
I want to perform in the 1984 Christmas edition
of Top of the Pops.
I want to be in Frankie Goes to Hollywood.
I want to be in the band.
I want to have a special rider:
shots of Baileys and deep-fried Spam.
I want to believe in the Power of Love,
not the one by Celine Dion.
I want to keep the vampires from your door.
Did I mention I hate *The S*n?*
I want to be in Frankie Goes to Hollywood.
I want everyone to survive HIV.
I want to be Holly Johnson,
just coz he inspires me.

EARTH

it feels boyish to put fingers in dirt-clay
with the class ma ch ch ch sheen of fat, pink worms
swallow, the idea of revolution, semen
the breast bone, the carcass of the factory chicken
make a wish, split yourself in two
I was in the Brownies
I was leader of the Pixies
six do-gooding girls
dance, monkey, dance
my second-in-command is a detective
now in the Greater Manchester Police force
fat green snakes sprout from my scalp
handcuff me to a tree
runway 3, HS2
they try to drown us in rules

BRAIN SENRYU III

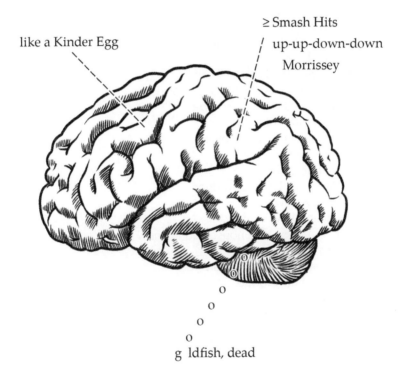

like a Kinder Egg

≥ Smash Hits
up-up-down-down
Morrissey

o
o
o
o
g ldfish, dead

FRAMED

Do the bones of this house
hate me? In the bathroom
the plaster is bare on one wall
in the shower; like cloud-spotting
it's a portrait gallery – the golem,
lady Mona of the manor,
orange Jesus. Do the bones
of this house hate me. Chewing gum
igloo stuck inside her
dressing table. Cat hair everywhere.
The house choking and coughing
on dead skin cells.
I shed a thousand skin cells an hour.
She sells skin cells on that sad shore.
The blade of the pencil sharpener.
There are three of us.
Slattern, slovenly, slut-mother.
A scrubber who doesn't
scrub-a-dub-dub.
The blood tie. The blood dries
quick quick slow,
quick quick slow.
Spinning, I hope that houses don't know
anything about mothering,
but then the house has seen
everything I have done
for these kids.
I only ever slapped the dog.
Surely the house knows
I had to be both good and bad cop.
Did I make this house a prison?
Did I make this house a hotel?
Did I make this house a hovel?
Did I make this house her hell?

Do the bones of this house

miss the stories from picture books?
Does the house miss the hugs?
Do hugs generate a spiritual energy
a bit like Vicks VapoRub?
Meditate, bitch.
You are fucking things up.
In the bathroom, remove your glasses,
that classic space for mothers, safe.
The windowsills were once painted green.
Everything stripped out and rebuilt.
The only thing left is guilt.

WISH I WAS PAST-AH

oh! that spaghetti
looks like
the hair
from the shower
they're
chasing me
the ghosts
looping into
the silver-head colander
lying amongst the minced meat
in the face-sized plate
you're a cheap mother
they say
you're doing it wrong
they say
20% fat/Aldi Price Match
leave me alone
daughters
daughters
daughters
spin and cross myself
just let me eat
or weep
in peace

HUB 101: HUSTERA

I stim the cheat key. I wait for him. I am almost certain
that I am in love. I have mainlined a sticky mix of
chemical dopamine, norepinephrine time and pheny so
many times it's a boring bit of the joblob. Lobotomise
me. The sticky levers of the typewriter tapping away at
my neurotransmitters, hacking out a story to make the
stuff while the punters leech it out. Symbiosis. I am a
sort of mother. Or an optic. They drink from me through
a straw. Take take take. I get a ssshadow of the feeling at
Sirens and here it is. IRL. Organic. A huge slug of it. Full-
fat feeling. The shots are on me. And for the first time I
miss the womb. I miss sacrificing it to save myself. Inside
my skinsewt the other organs roided up, full gourds,
body for hire. And in return I gave them the pear.

BABY

Let me tell you about the heartbeats,
streets of drowned suns,
slipping down the grid.

Ballistocardiograms,
Callisto, Myth,
in the lists of names
in this womb,
the wild moon of your mothership.

We thought you were a boychild,
little alien fur child,
little monkey brain.
Your heartbeat under 140 beats per minute.
We seen it on the ultrasound.
Half-listening to a podcast where a poet
said that everything can be described as a moon.
The scan picture mottled and futuristic.

Fast-forward. You're
free swimming, strip off next to the canal,
tightrope yourself on
the balance beam of the lock,
dive in, your stick-and-pin tattoos glistening.
Destiny written on your forearm.
Empty cans floating like ducks.
Empty hands don't give a fuck

and the drowned streets are
the best landlords ever.
Lock in, locked on,
your heartbeat, brains
like a little bath bomb fizzing.
Whizzing. This is the spinning future.

You are wild and free.
You are wild and free.
You are the reflection in the pink moon.
Look at me.

Look at me.
I am just a mother, an onlooker
of the pleasure-pain response.
A pinch of hedonism
and line full of clothes
bought from the charity shop,
the heartbeat slows,
sews stitches,
doesn't stop.

UNPACKING

At home, I looked about myself –
I've forgotten something.
Maybe it was misplaced or thrown away
in some mad lockdown clearance;
maybe I'd sent it to
the great charity shop in the sky
to die

and packed instead frayed
camping chairs and Lidl noodles
and oodles of insect repellent
I did not end up needing
for the festival
because the only thing that needed to feed
was something lost inside –
maybe it's my inner child?

And so we arrived in field and forest and played
red and orange ukuleles and learned a new song
where the magic porridge pot overflowed
(and the good toilet block did not,
stop, pot, stop) because something fairytale
had grown from the earth.

The Woodcutter's got a bass,
Granny's on the synth,
Wolf on drums, of course,
and Red Riding Hood
has blossomed
into a wild raspberry woman
with sequins on her face
and teeth vibrating with witch melodies,
spinning and grinning and beginning
to live again.

We watched Hare jump over the moon,

saw Artemis' wings, twit twoo,
then I found it!
On the first night away from home,
squashed like a sock
at the bottom of my sleeping bag,
a glitter shedskin,
and I stepped in,
iridescent, rose-tinted,
almost free.

SIX WAYS YOUNG HUMANS WITH ACNE-SPATTERED FACES CAN SAVE THE WORLD

·   these nihilistic children in politics
expected to save us, sit anxious round tables
welcome to your summer holiday art provision
these nihilistic children in politics, in 1819
would have been working or wed
she is fourteen, nuclear fission for a head
I am woman, hear me spore, brought in to inspire
live fast, die young, I whisper-wise to dot-dash blinking eyes
through my surgical mask
can I ask you to consider the magic of mushrooms?

SPOKE 669: DREAMSPEECH

It is an honour for me to be here with you today. Together we are making a difference. Humanity is now standing at a crossroads. We must decide which path we want to take. What do we want future living conditions for all species to be like? We will never stop fighting, we will never stop fighting for this planet and ourselves, our futures, and for the futures of our children and our grandchildren. Britain is a land where people go hungry. It's a hunger we can't really name. The sachets and the knock-off sweets fill one little whole up, but what is missing? We don't even know how much we've lost. My chest is a fricking spaghetti colander. And the Authority making Synth worms to weave through. Where is the sky? Where are our dreams?

WELCOME TO WONDERLAND

It was raining apples and oranges last night.
A spider diagram crept into my daughter's bedroom.
She was almost asleep, the blue
screen flickering, LOADING LOADING.
It attached itself to her wide open
MIND BLOWN
a bit like that facesucker from Alien
and awake she dreamed;

she was a superhuman brainbox,
leaping from her Grandma's brown couch
to swim in a ball pool of
amoebas and small, square phones,
PAAARTAAY this is living.
She is dancing with her very first car;
the Ford Fiesta and her are barebolt necking,
fizzing at the terminals.
The TV mast on Winter Hill,
like a benevolent grandad Alan Turing,
is beaming. She is
coding, computing, exploding.

Apple is not the only fruit, I tell her,

slice the frontal lobe of the orange,
gently blow the human fruit flies away.
Look closely and can you see
the scalpel shape of the tree?

Have you seen those aerial photos of mountain ranges
and the maps of rivers taken by drones?
Z marks the spot.
They show us we are all the same shapes
reflected in shapes reflected in
the wonder of this world.
Welcome to Wonderland.

Supersentient.
Free love in the garden.

It was raining apples and oranges last night.
The matrix dropped from its web.
My daughter killed it
with some hair spray and the heel of her heart.
I am horrified.

She resurrects it, her new tech-teddy,
rewires it, reboots it and us
with the wildness of AI
and newhardspun stories.
New. New. New. I knew.
Aye, the orange doesn't fall far from the tree.

ACKNOWLEDGEMENTS

Cover artwork by Lo Cole
Brain artwork by Peter Kennedy

The Kitchen Stinks appeared in SOAPBOX zine, edited by
Matt Abbott.
O-PEN was a commission for the launch of the Open
Music Archive and 'Together We Move' exhibition at
Salford Museum.
Tailor It appeared in 'The Tale of a Few Cities' exhibition at
Washington Arts Centre.
HUB 001: Headspace was published in PPRG Journal 2 at
Edge Hill University.
Earth and *Six Ways Young Humans With Acne Spattered
Faces Can Save The World* were commissioned poems as
part of a 10:1 dancepoetry film 'The Book of Witchin' in
response to art exhibition 'These Lancashire Women Are
Witches in Politics' by Anna FC Smith and Helen Mather.
Welcome to Wonderland was a commission for AL+ AL
and The Fire Within, Wigan for the launch of 'We Will
Always Be Together xx' art exhibition.